WHISPERS OF THE HEART

WHISPERS OF THE HEART

Teachings from Isram

Channeled by
Mara Joyce Chapel

ISBN: 1517724074

ISBN 13: 9781517724078

Acknowledgments and Gratitude

Many people inspired, encouraged and helped me write this book, and I thank each one for having faith in me. Without the following people in my life, this book would never have happened.

Charlotte S. Hunter, my dear spirited friend of many years, you were there from the very beginning with your tireless support and dedication. As *Whispers of the Heart* took shape over many days and nights you were there, pen in hand writing down Isram's every word. You are a free spirit with a profound curiosity and understanding of the Beyond, a teacher, healer and giver who has dedicated a great part of your life to the children of Africa. With your passion and love, you have created a better world for these precious children in so many ways. You always follow your heart and you will remain in my heart forever.

Lynne Guerra, writer. I thank you for giving me the creative concept and form of this book and allowing Isram's words to flow so beautifully. You are sorely missed.

In memory of LD Brodsky, poet, author, editor. I thank you from the bottom of my heart for your precious time, inspiration and for encouraging me to complete this book. I thank you for the many edits and how you loved what Isram had to say. I wish you were here to share the joy of this book. You would be so proud!

Kathleen Hughes, editor. I am so grateful that we had the chance to work together in the final stages of, *Whispers of the Heart*. You have brought the completion of this book to life. Thank you!

Linda Green and Denise Glatzer, my two wonderful sisters, you have always been there by my side through thick and thin. Although we are on very different paths, we have a common bond and understanding that can never be broken. We've shared hard times and good times, and I believe we know and trust that we will be there for each other no matter what. I love you both.

Kenneth R. Kafka, M.D., what can I say about what you have meant to me? There aren't many doctors like you: your devotion, caring and expertise as a doctor and friend are rare and special. You have always been there to ease my fear and point out what is real and what is not. You are sensitive, intuitive and strong, and I am lucky to have you in my life. Thank you for everything you have given me.

Judith Schmidt, Ph.D., my teacher, my cousin, my mentor. How can I ever thank you enough for all you have taught me, for the shining example you have been and continue to be in my life? You have always been there through thick and thin and words cannot express my gratitude and love. Because of you, I learned to open my heart when it was closed. When I didn't want to see or feel, you inspired me to go deeper, to look within. You will always be a part of me and I thank you for everything you are.

Jimmy Chapel, you are the light of my life. Your patience, compassion, encouragement and beautiful smile carry me every day. Your strong spirit shines bright inside and out. You are my healer, my friend, my husband. You have taught me many things with your steady understanding. You support me in everything I do and I will always be eternally grateful for your precious love.

Isram, I thank you for choosing me to be the channel for your words of wisdom. I had no idea what I was in for when you first appeared to me. The information I received was far beyond anything I could ever imagine. Your guidance, support and love carried me through the wonder and my questioning if this is real or not, and each and every lesson along the way unraveled another layer and a deeper understanding of the Divine and beyond. I am forever grateful for your words of wisdom, and that you have shared these words with so many, many people in times of despair and in times of joy. You have shined your light on me and I am truly blessed.

Introduction

I feel I have always been creative and spiritual. Perhaps I was born into these two worlds, because I can't remember a time when I wasn't thinking about an Eternal Life or singing, dancing, acting and performing in this life.

My childhood was not the norm. My mother, who was completely enthralled with show business, owned a dance and music school and was a "stage mother" who lived her passion through my sisters, Linda, Denise, and me. At four, I took singing, dancing, piano and acting lessons. By eight, I was in The Mace School for "young professionals." At ten, I auditioned for TV programs, commercials and musical theater, and at 14, I landed my first major show, *Bye Bye Birdie*. I graduated from a show business high school, Quintano's School for Young Professionals, and I must say, normal or not, I loved my life!

Growing up in show business, my classmates and friends included Patty Duke, Gregory Hines, and Bernadette Peters. We were a tight-fit family, only eight to a classroom, and our time in school was unique. We were in class from 10 to 1pm, and then were off to our singing, dancing and acting lessons and auditions, and in addition to school and classes we were all involved in television or Broadway shows, movies, commercials or modeling. To this day, many of us are still in touch with each other.

After graduating, I continued auditioning and performing and knew performing was what I wanted to do with my life. My career flourished as I performed in the national touring company of *Grease, Jesus Christ Superstar,* and many other exciting productions. I then became the assistant director to producer Nick DeNoia for a musical revue called *Broadway Tonite,* and eventually became sole producer of this show that tours the world to rave revues. I also produced special musical production numbers for major corporate functions and conventions.

Over the years as I developed my professional life I also nurtured my developing spiritual life. As a child growing up in New York City, I always felt somewhat different. I was fun and outgoing, but also very introspective. I sensed I had something deep inside I didn't see or recognize in other people. When I was little, I remember falling asleep every night thinking, "Okay, you die, we all die, but for how long, a month, a year, ten years, a hundred, a thousand years?" And as I kept thinking about this puzzle, I had a vision. I saw a spiral that went on forever, an Eternal Spiral, and I realized very young there was more to life than everyday life, the life we can see, taste, touch and hear.

And so my spiritual journey began very early. It seems that all my life I have been curious about all things "unseen," all things mystical and Divine. But it was when I was in my 20's that the spiritual world opened wide to me during a visit with my cousin Judy in San Francisco. I came down with the flu and Judy suggested I read the book, *The Only Dance There Is,* by Ram Dass. With every word I realized, this is what I had been looking for all my life!

I decided then and there I had to find Ram Dass. I had to talk to him, but about what I had no idea! I felt pulled into his world, drawn to him. I knew I had to meet with him. So when I returned to New York City, I tracked him down. I heard he went to Hilda's Friday night meditations, but he wasn't there. Then I discovered he was involved with the Hanuman

Foundation on Riverside Drive in Manhattan, but I couldn't get an appointment with him. Finally, desperate, I told his secretary, "You don't understand, I NEED to see Ram Dass!" Finally, she set up an appointment!

I was so excited on the day I would finally meet Ram Dass. My dream was coming true! As I walked up Riverside Drive to my appointment, I wondered what I was going to say to him. A million things went through my mind: "How can I impress him? What should I say first? What should I ask him?" Finally, I was in the sitting room waiting for him when he walked in and introduced himself. We went into a simple meditation room and he asked if I wanted a chair or if I would rather sit on the floor. I chose the floor.

We sat cross-legged opposite each other in silence and then he asked me how he could help me. I forgot everything I had rehearsed and rambled on about a million different things for the next twenty minutes. I talked about my mother, my father, my sister, my boyfriend, my this, my that. When I finally took a breath, Ram Dass said, "Are you through?" Only then did I realize I'd been talking a mile a minute and it was all nonsense. I looked at Ram Dass, "I sound like a fast-speed recording that never stops!" He said, "Yes, you do." And after a moment of silence, he asked me to breathe in and out of my heart as he placed his hand on my heart chakra, and at that moment everything became very still. It was a very special moment. Then Ram Dass told me I could go very far and asked me if I wanted to study with him. I couldn't believe it, but that moment was the beginning of a whole new world for me.

Later Ram Dass introduced me to a very special teacher and friend in my life, Soma Krishna (Judith Stanton) and I attended her weekly meditations on the upper east side in NYC for many years. This is where I met my spiritual family. We would gather after meditation class, and Ram Dass often joined us. It was an enriching and enlightening time full of laughter and good conversation.

Ram Dass was a great mirror for me, and I will be forever grateful for having him in my life and for all the wonderful people he introduced into my life. Thus began my years studying with many spiritual teachers and absorbing everything they taught me.

Time went on and one dark night I found myself in the middle of a spiritual crisis. Troubled, I started writing to God in my journal. I wrote every day for a month. Then one day my hand just flew across the page as I wrote word after word not knowing where these words were coming from. Clearly, they were not from me. After eight pages of "automatic writing" with ideas that startled me, whoever was writing through me said he had been watching me since I was a child and knew I was now ready to receive his teachings. Then he signed off with the word LOVE.

Not long after this, on a cold, snowy day in New York City, walking to my car on my way to meditation class, I heard a gentle whisper in my ear saying, "Never put down any level of Love because Love is the essence of the Universe. Everyone yearns to be loved." What?! I didn't know what to think about this whisper, so I just got in my car, turned on the engine and sat there polishing my nails while waiting for the car to warm up. But again, I heard the whisper. "Please put that away. I'm not finished." Startled, I sat up and listened to the whispers tell me more about Love. When this voice was finished, he said, "I bid you farewell and will meet with you again."

That was how it all began. In time, Isram began not only speaking to me, but also speaking through me with daily lessons and guidance. He explained how I was to use his Beautiful Teachings and told me I was the perfect channel for him because we had Compatible Energy. Now, when Isram speaks through me in a group, or in a private session, he touches each and every person exactly where they are, at their level of understanding so they can bring forth the very best in themselves, so they can recognize and embrace the Divine within them, or as he says, "The Isram within." He told me "Isram" means I Am, I am of God, I am of Love, and he told me he would be with me forever. All I have to do is listen.

How have I lived my spiritual life and show business life side by side? For me, it has sometimes felt like I was split between the two until I realized we all have many different facets to our lives, but they are all Divine. So the split between my spiritual life and the rest of my life has finally come together. Now instead of thinking that my career and my Spiritual life are separate or that "This is Holy and this is not Holy," I have come to see our whole life is Holy, every facet, all parts. As we follow our passions, and use and develop our talents and gifts, I believe we are always following The Divine.

It is my hope this book introducing Isram and his teachings will help others find their own Light, Strength and Truth. My wish is that with Isram's wisdom you, Dear Reader, can trust who you truly are and embrace and develop all your God-given gifts and talents. My hope is that you will use these Beautiful Teachings to connect with that special, quiet place within and listen to your true voice, the Voice of God within you.

What I Believe

I believe God, The Divine, our Higher Power, The Universe, The Force, whatever we call the Spiritual Power in our lives, is based on Divine Principles and Divine Intentions that apply to every aspect of our lives. Our dedication and commitment to whatever we do in life is our spiritual practice. How we apply our life lessons to become more conscious of our truth, talents and gifts, how we live our life, whether we're meditating, singing, selling or teaching, is all part of our Divine Practice.

As you read this book, please use the words and images you feel most comfortable with in your own spiritual life.

Contents

A Message from Isram

I am a teacher, of Light and Love. As a teacher, I enter into the souls of those who will accept my gentle Love, wisdom and compassion. Perhaps my teachings are a little strong at times, but they are always derived from Love.

I channel through a being named Mara Joyce Chapel, whom I have watched since she was a child. I teach Mara and others to identify their Divine Essence in a world often filled with pain and suffering, a world I believe can yet be transformed and fully realized at any given moment.

And so, my friends, I ask for acceptance into your hearts and minds so we may unite in Love, understanding and compassion, throughout and across the universe.

In Love and Light,

Isram

How to Use this Book

This book is organized around 18 Lessons, each one followed by a Meditation. Each lesson is coordinated with a meditation to allow you to move deeper into your understanding of the Lesson. Remember, with the act of Meditation you are expanding your awareness of how to use these teachings to transform your life and move beyond your limitations. The Meditations will deepen your understanding of what you read and allow you to practice using the teachings in your everyday life.

Meditation offers you the opportunity to practice stillness, to look within, to see beyond and increase your understanding of True Divine Guidance. Meditation will deepen your awareness of how to live a more joyous, prosperous and meaningful life.

To begin your reading and meditation, find a quiet place away from everyday distractions where you can create a sacred space, a space that will allow you simply to BE. Find a quiet corner in your life, a place of solitude, peace and comfort. Claim this time and space for your spiritual practice.

In this place, be still, breathe deep, relax and go within. Sit with your book, a cup of tea and the sense of quiet all around you and within you. Then begin to read the lesson, slowly, letting these beautiful teachings drift deep into your heart, mind and soul. Perhaps read and re-read the lesson as you quietly contemplate the meaning and feeling of Isram's words. When you are ready, read the Meditation, following the guidance there. Consider how, in meditation, you can practice these teachings in your everyday life.

After you have worked through the whole book, place it by your favorite chair or on your bedside table within arms reach for daily renewal. Then watch how your life changes and transforms as you make the Divine Power in these principles, lessons and guided meditations a deep and real part of your life.

Whispers of the Heart

Reaching out for God
is finding God.
Helping yourself and others
is finding God.

The only Truth
you can see right now
is the truth
you are able to understand.
But mind you,
it is not
the Ultimate Truth.

The blinders come
when you need to be in control.
You see, when you need
to be in control
you think it is
power and leadership.

On your plane you give
over control to a leader.
Where I exist, there is no such
thing as leadership as you know it.
We are one with the Divine,
the ultimate truth.
In this truth, there is no control.

What is most important is to have
a teacher who is a mirror of truth.
That is a true leader, one who serves
Divine Truth

When you recognize
the Truth in another,
you yearn for that Truth.
But if you look at others as leaders
you might follow them
and give them all your power
because you think
they have something you do not have.

It is better to simply let others
be a reflection
of Your Own Light, Love and Truth.

Hear and trust that The Divine
is within you.

Know that The God within you
is the most urgent and necessary
gift you can accept.

Whispers of the Heart
Meditation

As you sit comfortably, know there is a teacher in all of us,
a Divine power within all of us
wanting to express and share our deepest truth.

Bring your attention to when you were a small child,
nurtured and loved, nestled and caressed, held in the arms of those who
cared and surrounded you in love.
Allow yourself to remember.
Please imagine this nurturing love, even if it did not happen.
Absorb, breathe it in, breathe in and breathe out,
and feel and embody those tender moments.

Now see yourself in kindergarten learning your ABC's.
Your teacher is also nurturing and loving as she helps you
absorb your new lessons, your new realizations.
But then, remember a different feeling, at a different time
when you may have been told,
"You are wrong, everything you are doing is wrong!"
"This is the way you are supposed to do it."
Hear these words and breathe slowly and calmly.
Take yourself back to that time or person
when you were made to feel wrong.

Stay in that very moment, the moment that took away
your innocence and purity, the moment that made you
fight back to gain control.

Let yourself sit with these feelings.
Realize this was the important point
where you learned people could control you, and you could be
controlling yourself. Feel the conflict, the control.
Feel how you learned to communicate in an angry way,
in self-defense, in a self-righteous, controlling way.

Take a deep, gentle breath and picture yourself now communicating
with a loved one, a child, a friend, a teacher.
Breathe in and breathe out through your heart,
know you have a choice in how you communicate
your deepest Truths, to yourself, and to all others.

Understand you can choose to communicate without defensiveness.
Know you will never need to control others
or prove yourself again.
Acknowledge it is possible for you to simply Be;
Be in that place, Be with that person, Be in that conversation,
simply Be there, with no need to control what happens.

Embrace this Teaching. Breathe in. Breathe out. Stay quiet.
Embrace this Truth within you. Breathe in. Breathe out.
Embrace the part of you that wishes to speak your Truth
and express your beauty and Love.

Return again and again to this meditation to consciously practice
the principle of "Wisdom of Communication."
As you practice, may the words you choose to speak
always come from
the power and strength of The Divine.
May you become more conscious and aware,

through your meditation, of knowing exactly when
you are controlling and when you are not,
and how this powerful knowledge can change your life.

For what I am is in you.
For what you are, I am.
And together, we are One.

Channeling

It is important
to explain about the ego, and the material,
especially when
presenting them
from a Higher Level.
It is important
to put them aside,
and yet make them tangible
so you can understand
how to make them
available
to use at the proper time.

It is important that one knows how to step aside,
learn to listen,
and learn to accept the Higher Self,
whether you call it God,
Spirit,
Light,
or Love:
It is an existence of Pure Truth.

When and if you learn to listen
to the Truth,
you will receive
clarity and direction
for everything available
to you.

It cannot be too much.
It cannot be too little.
You are It,
and you will become One
with the Divine
as you integrate all
that is available to you
in this lifetime.

I do not say this is easy.
I do not say
you will not struggle.
You may stumble
and fall at times
as you allow yourself,
through practice,
through Love
and through anger,
to heal.

You will begin to understand,
you will begin to love,
and you will begin to learn
about the ego,
the mind,
the heart,
about struggle and prosperity,
aspects and dimensions,
which were unclear before,
through your very own compassion and willingness.

I say practice, listen to and trust
all that comes to you.
You must question and feel,

then you will know and
you will learn your Truth,
the Truth for you and you alone.
You must not compare.
You must not judge.
Only listen,
listen, listen,
or the lesson will be lost.

Channeling
Meditation

Let us sit comfortably, contemplating the connection of the mind,
body and spirit in each and every one of us.
Become aware of your Body, your Mind, your Spirit
as you open to Divine Guidance, bringing your attention to
the Heart Chakra, the heart of love, the seat of compassion.

Now, sense your heart and what it feels.
It can feel tight, or it can feel open, it can be constricted
or it can be free.
You can close your heart to others, or you can open your heart
to the whole world.
Keep your attention on your heart center,
for it is the Pathway to The Divine.

Breathe in, breathe out, watch the breath.

Breathing in, breathing out,
know that The Heart Chakra is important because
you will always feel the Truth here.
Your heart will tell you if you are out of alignment,
or if you are in fear, or if you are beautifully open to everything.

Be still and listen to your heart.

Next, bring your attention to The Crown Chakra,
at the top of your head. This is your connection between

Heaven and Earth, from Heaven to Earth, from Earth to Heaven.
This Chakra is The Divine Conduit allowing Divine Energy
to flow into your heart and spread freely throughout your
entire being.

This is the pathway to the Beyond.
But when your crown and your heart
are closed, you cannot give or receive.
So be aware of these two very important chakras
as you breathe in through the crown
and down to the heart,
then breathe in through the heart and up through the crown.
As you become very still, as you become very quiet,
as you open yourself in devotion to The Beyond, please
feel yourself receiving all that is Divine and Divine only.

For we do not touch this work unless it is Divine, of Love, of God,
of Divinity and Purity.
We use this powerful meditation to open the channel
between you and The Divine.

Each and every one of you has the capacity
to access The Beyond in this way.

Please do this for at least ten minutes.
And when you have time, spend more time with this Meditation.
Feel the opening of your senses, the clearing of this pathway.
Follow the flow of Energy.

Our intention is to see Beyond, to hear Beyond,
to feel Beyond, to know and sense The Beyond,
and yet to be present,
to Be in the here and now, to Be in this moment.

Over time, through your dedication
and devotion to Meditation, you will access more and more and more.

You will come to identify, understand and know
when you are moving from the ego to your expansive Divine Self.
For there are no limitations of the mind.
There are no limitations of the heart.
There are no limitations of The Beyond.

Everything is available and accessible
to each and every one of you.

And so, be the channel you desire to Be,
if you desire to be, for here is where the work
is of utmost importance.
It Is, and you are It.

How far do you want to go?
How open do you want to be?
How much information do you want to access and receive?
Breathe gently and release. Very gently. Very gently.

Breathe into this meditation to open the channel to The Divine.

The key is Awareness, Awareness. Awareness of here,
now and Beyond. Awareness.
To be Aware, breathe gently and release.
Let yourself feel the tightness and release it.

With each release, you expand.
Breathe in, feel the tightness, let yourself expand a little more.
Then breathe out and slowly come into the present.
Be present. Breathe. Release.

So, this is where we start; this is the key,
this is how to open, how to Be a channel.

Now, as you move through these exercises and meditations,
use all these simple tools. They are available to use
for each and every one of you.
The tools are endless, as you touch, tap and radiate
the Divine Gift within you,
the treasure chest of wisdom and Divine Knowledge.

There is no easy way.
This is The Way.
To sit. To breathe. To Be. To learn to open.

Whether your Spirit Guide talks to you
or whether the knowing comes through your heart
or your writing, or whether you see through your Third Eye,
these are your gifts, your promises fulfilled.
They are here, there, always. They are nothing new.
The only thing new is your access to them and
your ability to receive these gifts of wisdom.
Now, become the channel you are, Divinely and rightly so.
Please make this a conscious meditation throughout the day.
Be aware of your every breath. Be aware of your body.
Be aware of your heart with every encounter you have,
every situation, every person.

Be aware of the Dimension beyond the everyday
while you are in the everyday.

Through your breath, you can journey to The Beyond
at any time, in any moment.

You can journey there, tap into the great wisdom
and become the channel you desire to be.
And so I bless you, bless you, bless you, always.
Blessings and farewell.

Pain to Change

Let us go into the depths of your being,
to where pain finds a home
and anger screams or is silent,
a place where feelings
tend to curl up within.

You have become accepting of this place.
You have given this place over to
all your negative thoughts and feelings,
sent them there to live, sleep
and act out.
And so you do not recognize
what is going on in this place deep within.

How could there be no pain,
How could there be light,
How could there be love,
when you have given such permission
to the fire,
and the anguish,
to the disease and the distorted?

So, herein lies your work
and your choice:
to look at and confront,
to heal and to love.

Your work is cut out for you.
The Light exists,
if you wish to see it.
The Love remains,
if you wish to be it.
In all its peace
and in all its joy.

So ask yourself;
why is my life
so difficult and painful?
Why am I so miserable?
Why can't I deal with it?
Why do I want to die?
Is this the way
Life is supposed to be?
Do I have a choice?

Let us understand
how the desire to die,
comes not from a desire
to let go of the physical.
It comes from a desire to change
and to release your pain.
It comes from a desire to heal and to see.
It comes from a desire to love.
It comes from a desire
to live.

I encourage
each and every one of you
to laugh and not be afraid of your own power.
There are many teachings
and tools to help you along The Path.

Again, I encourage you to move on through your strength,
your love and your courage.
Recognize, caress and adore the Loving Being
you truly are.

If you make a choice to do the work,
if you take the actions,
if you allow yourself
to receive the promises of God,
each and every one of you will heal within.

Pain to Change
Meditation

Sit comfortably bringing your attention to any place
that may be painful for you. It may be a sad place,
a hurtful or dark place, a heavy place keeping you in bondage,
keeping you from seeing the Light.
Enter this place and know you are safe in this very moment.
Gently move through the darkness here, and I promise you,
under the dark, there is Light.
Feel what is held in this place for you.
Are you sad, anxious or fearful? These feelings may be
stopping you from moving out into the world
to achieve what you envision for your life.

If you encounter fear, just breathe gently. Very gently.

Breathe in and breathe out. Breathe in and breathe out.
Sit with these feelings, and by doing this daily meditation
you will see darkness is only energy,
only a shadowy energy where God needs to enter,
where Light needs to shine.

And so now, envision a white light entering this place,
a Divine flash of Light embracing the darkness.
Let this Light surround you, enter every part of your Being
and light up every cell in your body.
Sit in this Divine Light, awash in God's Love, secure in the Light
of a Higher Power, that banishes all darkness.

Breathe in and breathe out.
There is nothing to fear and nothing to hold you down.
Now you become more,
more and more yourself in ever greater ways.
With higher thoughts and actions, you see the great Being
you already are. You see the Self the darkness was hiding.
And so I Bless you for now and always.

Healing Light

The Light magnifies
and the Light reflects.
If you are conscious,
open and receptive
to the Light,
you can be healed,
instantaneously.

However,
you must understand
the process that exists
between the creation of fear
and the Healing Light.
When you are healed
by the Light, the Ultimate,
the Light of God,
your work
is the work that goes on
between the fear
and the Light.

Until you truly come to understand
what is Real,
as opposed to the illusions
you dream,
spider webs

will stand in the way
of your healing.

You must come to trust
that you are riding the elevator
to God's love,
where harmony, balance,
and truth await.

And you are all invited.

Healing Light
Meditation

Lie comfortably on your back, sink into a deep relaxation,
take deep, gentle breaths.

Bring your attention to the top of your head, the Crown Chakra,
and imagine a bright white Light entering your crown
and filling your entire body from head to toe.

Let this Divine Light melt your stress, anger and fear,
release all the tension in your physical body;
it is the Light of God.

Stay very conscious during this meditation,
Watch and observe where the Light travels within.

Now let your emotions melt and soften
through your gentle breath.
Then, once again, give permission for the Light
to run through your body, to continue to heal whatever it encounters.

Rest comfortably.
Then repeat and continue this meditation:

Relax, breathe, observe, release and bathe
in the Light of Love and Peace.

Shining the Light

Many of you
are developing,
becoming a channel
for the Light.
But just because you sometimes use the Light,
it does not mean
you don't have to always look within.
It does not mean
you do not have fear
or feel anger
or jealousy
or resentment
or any of the other earthly emotions.
It does not mean
your inner work is complete.

If you are able to see the Light,
it may be
a very clear tool
for you to work with.
But if you are developing your skills,
the Light may magnify issues
you are working on
in the moment.

If you are holding fear,
you will express and feel the fear.
In your reality
the fear is very real,
but the truth is,
fear will not support you in any way.
The truth is,
you give too much power
to fear.

There are many tools
you can use
in working with fear:
meditating,
praying,
or just talking about it.

However,
if you are working with Light,
you can use the Light
to penetrate
through fear like a laser.

Know that the Light
may also magnify the fear
three times as much.
When you turn
the Light on,
you will see
more vividly,
more clearly.

Continue
to let the Light
keep penetrating
through you.
Eventually,
it will embody
your whole being
and dissolve the fear.
There is nothing
more powerful
than Light,
for it is
the Light of God.

Shining the Light
Meditation

Sit comfortably with your eyes closed and let yourself see outward
to the trees, the leaves, the ocean.
Let yourself see the skies, the earth, the sadness and distortion.
See the world of beauty. See the world of darkness.
Let your eyes see a world of love and a world of sadness.
Allow, see whatever is in front of you.

Keep your attention on the outside world.
See shopping for food and clothing, buying a new home, a car.
Let your eyes see what is all around you.

Without judgment, see and be present.
Be still in your seeing and being.
Then, shine a light on everything you see,
light or dark.
Shine a beautiful light on everything you see all around you.

Relax. Sit comfortably, and now change your focus
from everything outside of you to what is inside.
Now look inward, focusing on your
Third Eye.
Breathe in and out.

Bring attention to all that is going on in your
inner life, your personal issues, health, finances and obligations
and breathe gently, just breathe.

And with all these issues, know you simply are.
You are present with them.
Don't run from them, don't fear them, just be with them.
Sit. Be. Breathe in and breathe out.

Feel the difference in the energy when you
focus outward, when you focus inward, outward, inward.

Now envision a light right in the center of your belly button.
Let this light become larger and larger and larger,
as large as it can be through your eyes.

Sit for a few moments, very conscious and very aware.
Feel the grandeur of your great and powerful being.
Feel your presence.

In this state, you can conquer anything.
For it is in this state that one can transform anything by choice,
by intention, by being in the Truth, by opening
your eyes and seeing beyond,
and experiencing what is available.

I give you a diamond to place in the center of your Third Eye.
Then gently with your right hand, take the diamond
and place it in your heart. Let this diamond magnify
all that you need to see and know.
For all your lessons are in the diamond.

Take a deep, gentle breath.

And so I bless you, bless you, bless you, for now and always.

Your Own Light

When you open to Divine Guidance,
you come to know
the Light,
you come to know Energy,
its direction,
its movement.

When you walk in the Light,
it might be a tunnel,
a ray,
or sunshine.

As you attune,
all things around you
become finer
and finer
and finer.

You allow
your whole being,
you allow your whole self,
to be moved by the Light.

As you develop,
you come to know
that you are

Divinely guided,
no matter
what the lessons
might be.

You consciously develop
the knowing and trust,
as you walk the path.

When you fall down
do not fret,
do not fear.
Right at that moment,
your lesson appears.

If you recognize the lesson,
you have returned,
without guilt,
without fear,
without anger.
You have returned to the Path.
You are back on the Path.

Do you think
you are walking alone?
Do you think
you are controlling
the Path you walk?
No.
No.
No.
That is impossible.

As you tune into the eons,
the Energy,
the Light,
the Truth,
all in the purest form you can imagine,
you tune into
Love.

When you
awaken to Truth
more
and more
each day,
you will say
yes
more than you will say
no.
You will say
yes,
again
and again
and
again,
until you feel it
deep within,
until you know it
to be true.
That is when
you truly walk
with the Divine,
in the Absolute.

Your Own Light
Meditation

As you sit in meditation, I want to say to you who are
delving into the spiritual world,
this is a world of love where you can actually live with love,
and be one with it as you come to understand there is no separation.
You are who you are,
as you learn to be in the world, in your body.

Embrace your spirit, embrace love, embrace all of who you are.
Through your work, writing, dancing, singing, cooking,
you are able to bring it all into that one melting pot.

This is my prayer for all of you that you do not separate anything,
that you live in your body, spirit and the greater mind of The Beyond,
all at the same time.
Please live where you can live a happy, rich life, in all ways,
without splitting, separating, without saying this is spiritual and that is not.

For you intuitively know right from wrong, you know the Law of God.
And so I ask you to come into the center of Light,
to the love of who you Divinely and rightfully are.
You are a shining Light, a shining star, each and every one of you.

Accept your own Light, walk the path with flowers surrounding
you and halos hovering over you.

Enter into a deep, loving space.
Take a moment to be quiet, be still and then feel,
sense and listen to your heart.

Now, watch your mind, and come back to your heart.
Let yourself shine. This is the true source of Light.
No need to manipulate, run or grab it.
Just let it be and let it flow through you.

Be it, be in it, walk, run, swim and grow in it;
it never dies and is always present.
Allow The Light to shine and to let you see.

The Light can magnify the beauty, grace and intelligence
of your gifts, and even the darkness within, which is not a bad thing.
Whatever place in your being needs to be looked at,
cleared and cleansed, let The Light shine there.

Breathe gently, softly and sweetly,
as you journey and move on.
Search and seek, always look for The Light in all things.
Look for The Light in each and every soul,
even through the darkness.
The Light is everlasting.

It might be hidden, but through your eyes, you can see Beyond.
Through your eyes, you can love a little more.
You have the capacity through your work, growth and dedication

to see the Light in everything.
Most importantly, see The Light within You.

Be The Light. Radiate The Light. Shine and Soar.

And so I bless you, bless you, bless you, for now and always.

Light
is the most powerful
source of Energy there is.
However,
when working with Light,
you are working with heat rays
and electrical energy.

As you direct the Light,
the being you are working with
must be open
and receptive.
He must have released
a certain amount of fear.
She must be existing
in a conscious
loving
energy.

The light
can penetrate
and heal
any tumor,
cancer,
or
disease.

The only problem is
that one must be ready
to accept the Light
of their own Divine Love.

When you are channeling Light,
you must be very careful
and conscious of
who you are working with,
because sometimes
the Light can be too strong
or overwhelming
for that person.

You must know
your own power and strength
as a channel.

Light is an electrical current
that is Everlasting.
It has a vibration of its own.
It can be seen and felt
by many.

It is the Light
that your soul,
sometimes like a shooting star,
passes through
at the moment of death.

Through the moments
of awareness

and developing,
you will learn
how to open your mind and body,
to receive
or to direct
the Light,
for either you
or for someone else.
Let
the
Light
warm you.

You cannot always consciously exist
in the Light,
because of the many purposes
for which you are here.

Most importantly,
you must learn
about the body,
the emotions,
the mind,
and the spirit.

As you develop,
you will sustain the Light
for longer periods of time.
Do not be alarmed
if you feel, at times,
that you cannot consistently hold

or channel the Light,
for
there
is
nothing
to
hold.

Healing with Light
Meditation

I ask you to sit comfortably and feel yourself open
as we share and talk about the importance of Light,
how fast Light travels, how powerful
it is, and how The Light can heal.

You must be very careful as a healer, aware, knowledgeable,
and understanding of how strong The Light is.
Know who you are working with, because Light is very powerful.

Sit comfortably. Stay open. Working with Light as a tool,
you will come to understand a little more
about your own insight and understanding of the power of Light.
Breathe gently and restfully, relax. Breathe gently and release.
You can direct The Light in many ways: touch, thought
and through the Third Eye.
You can even send Light across the country.
That's how powerful it is.
The speed of Light is faster than a blink of your eye.

You can touch somebody with your hand and penetrate the Light,
but when do you stop?
When do you know if it's too much or too little?
You will know only through your own development,
wisdom and understanding.
You can not know from the ego, because The Light is not from you.

The Light is from The Divine, from God,
from the most powerful Energy that exists.
You are simply a channel and through you
the Light can run very fast, or move slow.

It is possible to move the Light from side to side,
redirect it, move it up or down.
You can also pull the Light back.

Take your hand and hold it up, feel the heat in your hand
or pouring out of your fingertips.
Experience the Light moving out of your hand.

As a healer, it is important to know your own strength and intent.
Meditation and dedication are of utmost importance.
Especially if you are working with others during the healing process.

Breathe gently and let go. Breathe gently and let go.

Now mind you, healing can take place instantaneously.
If the receptor is saying yes, and is open, and is in true alignment
with
Divine healing,
there can be a miraculous healing.

It is important as a healer not to be disappointed
or feel you are a failure if the receptor is not open.
As a vessel, you are not the owner of the Light.
Nor do you have the power to manipulate Light.
If you try, you will just deplete your own gift.

Take a deep, gentle breath and release.
Now, bring the Light into your heart and breathe gently.
It is important to rest and rejuvenate.
Sitting in the Light and letting the Light engulf you,
is just letting it be.

This is quite different from channeling the Light into another being.
Moving and directing Light, you are moving in action.
You are doing, you are giving, so let's not get confused.

In the bigger picture, Light is Light and there is one Divine Light.
But, in your separation as human beings,
there are different levels and different lessons to work on, in
body, mind and spirit.

Sit gently and lovingly, and I hope this tool has been helpful for you,
especially for those who desire to live and dwell
in a great spiritual understanding and
use their gifts and talents in the greatest possible way.
And so I bless you, bless you, bless you, in light and love.

Uniting with God

What a pleasure it is to unite with God,
to unite in the Oneness,
to unite in the holiness,
and in your own holiness,
to dwell in peace,
to share in friendship,
to exist in love
and to share in love.

When you enter fear,
remember,
God is here.
He dwells
in you
and inspires you
and loves each falling tear.

So let the journey
you are on
be of great teachings:
listen to the lessons.

Unite with God,
because God is here.
Breathe in and out
of your heart chakra,
your heart that yearns,
your heart that desires,

your heart that longs
to be full and rich.

Yet always know
there will be
many distractions
trying to divert you
from all that you are longing for,
distractions
that will cause you to sink,
once again,
in pain,
in sorrow,
in hurt,
in doubt,
in fear.

It is then
that you must remember,
simply remember,
that God
did not go anywhere,
did not leave
you,
did not hide,
that God is within you,
right by your side.

Take a deep breath,
breathe in love,
release the fear.
Breathe in air,
for God is here.

Remember!
Remember!
Remember!
You are love.
You are one
with God.

Remember!

Uniting with God
Meditation

Sit, be comfortable and let God's Energy surround you
with no need to define or question.
Sit in the Divine, the wonder, the Love, the Perfection and Divinity.
Breathe gently, and feel God's healing Love within you and around you.

Tap the place within you that needs to be touched, healed and loved.
Staying focused on those areas, bring forth a beautiful White Light.
Picture the White Light swirling and nourishing each and every cell.

Breathe in and breathe out. Breathe in and breathe out.
Open to the wonder and the fullness of the Light.

Let the Light move and trickle through you.
Let it surround, caress and hold you.
Breathe gently, and with each breath
let yourself expand a little more, opening and closing,
opening and closing.

Know that the Divine presence of God is within you,
in your heart, your soul, your mind and Beyond.
Embrace God's gift of love within.
Embrace that which needs to be comforted.
Embrace those who you Divinely love.
Embrace those you love.
Embrace those who you struggle with,
and see Beyond.

God needs you and you need God.
The Divine is within you
and the Divine is God.
Perfection is perfection,
and perfection is God.
The Law of God is the Supreme,
the Divine, the Light and the Love.
Know that you are one. Know that you are united.

Carry this meditation throughout the day, in your mind, heart and soul.

The Healing Power Within

You must trust
the healing power
that is within you.
The healing power
energizes
every cell.
The healing power
runs through you.

Make the choice
to receive
this Healing Energy.

Can you accept
that each and every encounter
is an encounter
from which to learn,
while learning to love yourself?

When you are ready
to let your old patterns die,
you will come to believe
there is Light
after darkness,
there is laughter
after sorrow,

there is joy and
there is love,
there is compassion,
there is humanity and
there is integrity,
there is life
after life.

The Healing Power Within
Meditation

Let us sit for a moment to open to the Divine healing power within.
This is the place where Miracles happen,
a place that needs you to say yes, yes, yes,
I accept, I accept, without an inkling of a doubt.

If there is one thought of negativity or doubt, you will hesitate,
linger, and think you need to investigate.
But Healing is available to each and every soul
in a split second.

Let us simply, quietly look within and ask:
Am I ready for a miracle?
Am I ready to be healed?
Are my cells and thought patterns ready to shift?
Am I, in body, mind and spirit ready to transform?

There is no time limit. There is no I must do this today.

On your Spiritual Journey, as you meditate, contemplate
and write in your journal, please
look inside,
look through the diamond that magnifies all there is.
Know you can transform anything through willingness, readiness
and acceptance of your own Divine Being.

Sit quietly, searching:
What part of you is saying, "No I'm not ready."

What part is saying, "I can't let go."
What part of you is saying,
"I love him, her, but I'm so miserable."
What part is saying, "I hate my work."

So through your thoughts, feelings, perception and misconceptions,
these are your lessons.

As you sit in meditation, with issues going on in your life,
I ask you to put them to sleep for now,
just for a moment, this moment.
Know you won't be able to put them to sleep for very long
because they are integrated in your mind,
in your habits and in your very cell.

But right now, visualize yourself free as the wind,
laughing, singing, dancing, doing whatever you love to do.
See yourself in this moment of joy, where all is Perfect and Divine.
Hug yourself, for when you hug yourself, you say, Yes!
Love yourself, for once, love yourself and say, Yes!

Embrace yourself, for there is the possibility
in all of you for miraculous healing.

So, through time and understanding, by being present and open,
when you are not afraid to look within,
you can transform, shift and change;
inwardly and outwardly, you can change as you feed
and nourish yourself with all that is Good.

You will learn in time to move away from situations
that are harmful to you.
You will learn to rest with delight with those you love.

Sit for a moment accepting all the great possibilities
radiating through you.

I love you, love you, love you as you love yourself.

Reality

The breath of life
has no beginning
and has no end.

And so,
you observe your reality:
once again you
thought you knew it all.
Then what happened
to all
that you had placed
in perfect order?
This is the game of life.
You are the experience.

Until you truly allow yourself
to experience the Truth
which is already Divine,
you will seek and
you will search,
you will get it and
you will lose it,
you will find it and
you will fight it.

Until you are willing
to give up the fight,

until you are ready
and willing to surrender
into your greater
and deepest
knowing of the existence
of God.

Until you are able
to accept the radiance
of your own being,
until you are able to
allow the light within
to manifest
through every cell
and every thought,
you will search and
you will seek,
you will fight and
you will win,
you will lose it and
you will get it,
and you will destroy it.

Enter
into meditation,
seeking the Light
and Love
within,
seeking the truth
within,

which will free you
from the bondage.

I bless you,
bless you,
bless you.

Reality
Meditation

Reality is simply where you are, how you see things,
how you live your life and how you understand your life.
This is your reality.

Sit quietly and openly, accepting all you know,
all you understand, all you manifest.
This is your understanding.

Breathe gently, releasing the past without judgment.
There is no right or wrong, there is only embracing
everything in your life,
everything you have created.
This is your reality, the only reality you know.

Breathe in, now moving to accept a greater reality,
allowing yourself to open your eyes and your mind
and quietly within saying, Yes, Yes, Yes,
I accept.

I accept more Love. I accept Divine Guidance
to help me manifest,
create, be used as a vessel for a greater reality,
a greater understanding.

Breathe in the Divine. Breathe in the Greatness.
Embrace the gifts of God that reside in your mind, in your heart
and in your every cell.

Every level of reality is creation, and you are the creator.

Let this be your reality for today.
Blessings and farewell for now.

Be in The Light

Be in your star,
be in the now,
be in the present,
be the best you can be,
be awake
as much as you can;
then always practice
the best you can practice,
create the greatest of creations,
be in the abundance,
be in the fullness,
be the gentleness and
be the tenderness,
be the strength,
be the core,
be the vision,
be and live
the experience of life,
of love,
the experience
you allow yourself
to be in.

Remind yourself, remember,
and you will live in that experience
a little bit more
each day,

each moment,
each second,
throughout each thought.

This is not to say
you will not drop out
of the experience
of Love at times,
but if you keep reminding yourself
it does exist,
it is present,
then you will recognize it
more and more easily
than before.
Then,
if you drop out, again,
you will remind yourself, again,
to return.

At this time in the world,
with much devastation,
with much sickness
of the mind,
we need more Light,
more and more
and more,
each day,
each second,
and with each breath we take,
we need
to be in the Light of the world,
to be in the Light
for the others who are suffering.

Join with The Light.

You cannot say
you can or will
ever save anybody,
but you must try.
You can remember
and you can hope.

Be in the Being,
be in the Present,
be in the Light
and see the Greatness
from a greater perception
of the God Being.

For in the God Being
is your emotional being.
In the God Being
is your Love,
is your Light.
In the God Being
lies all of you,
and all is embraced,
and there is nothing
left out of that Being,
nothing.

Therefore,
the mind is cleansed,
the mind is healed,
in fullness
and in richness.

Have it all,
feel it all,
be it all,
in strength,
in power and
in truth.

You will keep saying,
yes,
more
and more
and more
and more,
as you keep proceeding,
and as you keep understanding,
you will become very clear
about the different levels
of the body,
mind,
and spirit.
You will come to know
there is no separation
between them.
None at all.

Be in The Light
Meditation

Bring the Eternal Light into the center of your being.
Recognize it, feel it, sense it.

Sit for a few moments with this Light,
as it grows brighter and brighter and brighter.
And the brighter it becomes, the larger it gets.
The larger it gets, the greater it spreads to the world
and throughout the universe, where it will touch many.

It is so important in your work and in your practice
that you share and live in this Light. That you recognize this Light,
that you emanate and radiate this Light through your being.
You are the savior. You are the saviors of this upside-down world where
you all exist.

If each and every soul can recognize this
and move this Light out into the world, touching those in darkness,
you are then saving your planet.

Breathe gently and recognize once again, this beautiful, beautiful
White Light growing larger and larger and larger.

Breathe in Love. Breathe out Love.

Now in your mind's eye, hold this White Light and consciously
send it out to the universe.
Once you release it, it will journey exactly where it needs to go.

Visualize this White Light once again,
in your mind's eye.
See a person you want to send this White Light to and
hold it, hold it, hold it...then
release it directly to that person. Let it go.

Come back to your mind's eye. Now direct the white light inwardly.
If there is a specific place in need of healing, send the light there.
For nothing is more powerful than light,
the Light of God.
It cannot be destroyed. It knows no destruction.
It is the almighty powerful Miracle.
Breathe in and let go.

Please practice this meditation throughout your day.
I ask you, please, to recognize this Light within you.

When you think of someone during the day,
take a moment and send them White Light.
Take a moment and send it out to your planet.
Take a moment and send it out to those who are suffering.
Take a moment and send it out to those who do not recognize the Light.
They may never recognize the Light, but you do, and the Light
knows exactly where to go.

Breathe in and breathe out. Be the Light. Be in the One.
Be in Love with The Light.

And so I bless you, bless you, bless you, for now and always.

Following the Energy

Let us talk
about staying in tune and
staying in the flow.
Let us talk
about energy
traveling through the body,
energy
sometimes known as anxiety
or sadness,
sometimes as joy
and laughter.
Let us become aware
and follow the energy
without going against it
and without manipulating it.

Paying attention
and following the energy
is what will lead you
to your lucky star.
It is important
that you stay very conscious
in whatever
you do.
If you are in the world,
be in the world.
If you are working on a project,
be in the project, consciously.

Be with the Energy,
in your full spirit,
even if you
experience anxiety
or excitement.

If you go grocery shopping,
delight in it, be conscious.
If you are meditating,
be in the meditation,
be conscious.

If you follow the stream,
and if you
keep the stream clear,
you can swim
through the waves,
you can
swim
through the calm sea
or the storm
or the ripples in the water.

You will swim to land,
to the sand,
to the sun,
to the trees
and to all that is of peace
and
of God and love.

So follow your heart
to that lucky star
and let that lucky star

reflect upon your heart.
Let your heart open
so you may see
the sun and moon and stars radiating
your whole being.

Following the Energy
Meditation

Let us meditate on following your energy.
Is your energy tired and sluggish or vibrant? Are there
other energies
tugging at you and draining you of your own energy?

Breathe, breathe, breathe, and with each breath re-energize yourself.

Your energy is boundless, endless and vital, but you must
align and nourish it within.

Paying attention, being conscious and
following your energy is the key.

Be conscious of your energy.
What is your energy's environment? What do you feel?
Is your energy healthy or does it pull, tug, drain you?

Breathe.

Your energy is a blessing. You must protect that blessing
and use it properly, use it wisely.

Awaken in every thought, every movement and every step you take.

For you are a shining star!

Enjoy and love.

What's Your Hurry?

What's your hurry,
my children?
Where are you going?
What are you doing?

Hurry to find the Light.
Hurry to make money.
Hurry to pay your rent.
Hurry to become whole.
Hurry to become spiritual.
Hurry to get ready for a date:
Hurry,
Hurry,
Hurry!

You must stop
for a moment,
my children.
You must stop
and realize that the Light
is already within.

Where are you going,
where are you hurrying to?
What are you grabbing onto?
What are you
trying to make happen?

Again,
may I say,
the Light already is.
It is not moving away from you.
It is not going anywhere.
No.
No.
No.

The question is,
are you turning away from the Light
and if so, where are you going?
Are you grasping and holding onto
that which separates you
from the Light?
Do you still hold onto fear
in the absence of Light,
in the absence of Love?

Although the absence of Light
is a darkness,
an emptiness,
it is also a place to dwell,
a place you have chosen;
and you can become very comfortable
in that chosen home,
all the while feeling miserable.
You can become very used to this place
and, perhaps, feel
this is all you deserve.

Oh no,
no,
no,

my children,
no,
no,
no.
It's just a tunnel
you walk through,
not a home to dwell in.
You need not worry
as you pass through that tunnel.
You need not run.

Use the Light
to see the absence of love.
The darkness you see
will not serve you,
if you cannot recognize the Light.
Therein lies love.

I invite you to
open and open slowly.
Feel your love.
Be that love.
Recognize your own Light and
laughter within,
for if you hurry,
you will miss
what's already there.
You will lose it.

Consciously now,
walk each step into the Light,
and do so with a willingness,
a desire to walk each step
towards God.

Stop!
Feel your feelings.
Look within.
Embrace yourself.
Take a step.
Look around you and
look at others,
look at their faces,
look at their pain,
look at their laughter
and their soft, gentle smiles
of love.

Let their smiles warm your heart.
Take another step.
Look around you,
see the pain,
the misery,
see their useless actions.
Stop in the center of it all
and connect with the Light.

Perhaps your Light can touch some of their misery,
heal some of their pain and anguish.
Feel your heart smile,
even though saddened.
Feel your Light.
See your Light.
Even though there may be
energies of darkness
around you,
you will be protected
by the Light.

Let your Light shine
around the darkness.

Take another step.
Look at the rainbow,
look,
at the rainbow.

And now,
where do you go,
what do you do?
Slow down to hear.
Slow down
to see Love.
Don't hurry.
Take your time
and give
someone
a helping hand, someone
who can't walk fast, who can't hurry.
Slow down to their pace.
Be conscious.
Share that space of love with them.
Share that space of love with yourself.
Walk in that space.
Cross the street.
You may start to walk
a little faster
or you may run.
But don't be
in too much of a hurry.
You may miss the rainbow.
You may miss the sun.

Stop.
Look at the sun and
look at the trees,
eat lunch,
go shopping and
meet friends.
Slow down. Stop.
Review the day.
Think of your friends,
with love.
Understand who they are.
Understand where they are.

Look at yourself.
Understand
who you are,
as much as you can.

Stop,
rest,
sleep in peace.
Awaken
to a brand new day
of sunshine.
Continue to grow.

Move in time,
space,
and harmony.
Move in balance
truth,
light,
and awareness.

Be love,
and love all that you do.
And so I say to you,
peace, peace, peace.

What's Your Hurry?
Meditation

Take a deep, gentle breath and let the sunshine in.
Let your heart sing. Let laughter prevail.

Sit quietly. Breathe gently into your heart chakra.
Envision a beautiful rainbow there. Sit in the middle of the rainbow,
centered, legs crossed and palms up, keeping the attention on the breath.

Inhaling one, exhaling two. Inhaling one, exhaling two.
Now, please bring your attention to your busy, busy day.
See yourself rushing to work, rushing to do this, rushing to do that,
running to go shopping, running late for an appointment,
running to make dinner,
running to meet friends,
rushing to meet a deadline.
Running, running, rushing, running.
So much energy used for rushing and running around and around.

Now quietly, breathing in and breathing out, bring your energy back
from all the rushing, bring it back and let it feed your soul.
With each inhalation and exhalation, feel yourself slowing down,
slowing down from your busy schedule, your busy day, your busy mind.
Allow this time for you to receive and center your energy.

Notice how, when you are rushed, you are pulled out of your body,
and how your energy changes as you rush and run.

Now, take a deep, gentle breath and come back to yourself.
Let your breath bring you back into your body, back into your energy.
Sense your energy within and how you can use and direct
this beautiful gift.

For the next ten minutes, sit centered in the rainbow,
watching yourself running through your day, then returning to your center.
See how when you are running, running, running, you run out of energy.
See how when you are sitting centered, you are receiving and
directing your energy.

Continue sitting comfortably.
Use this time to open and receive your energy:
You are now directing the energy, expanding your mind
and your awareness.

Please use this powerful meditation daily to gain great benefits; use it to
fuel your body, mind and spirit so your days will be filled
with all the energy you need.

Emptiness

You enter
into this world,
a world of love and fear,
joy and sorrow,
a world of fulfillment and emptiness,
laughter and tears.

Sometimes,
there is a sorrow
that settles within,
a sadness,
a loneliness,
an emptiness,
a cave.

Your parents
try to nourish this sorrow.
Laughter tries to nourish it.
Ice cream tries to nourish it.
But the world of sadness remains.

Your understanding
of love
tries to fill
a relationship,
a marriage.
You think and hope
there will be the answer.

But you continue to
live in a world of loneliness,
emptiness,
tears and frustration.
You go around and around,
trying to find
your way home,
trying to find
laughter,
joy,
harmony.
But you find
nothing.
Nothing, no one
can fill this empty cave.

Then two million dollars
comes your way,
but flies right through your fingers.
Where did it go?
What happened?
Two million dollars;
you were a millionaire!
Wasn't that what you needed?

The cave
is empty, once again.
You start to question deeply.
What's going on?
Who am I?
What am I?
Am I a child of God?
If so,

why am I
so unhappy?
If so,
why does God
not love me?
If so,
what am I to do?

You ask these questions.
You go around in circles.
You will go around
and around
and around,
until you stop, recognize,
and realize
there is a Calling,
there is a longing,
there is a God,
and God alone
is the only source
who can fill
this emptiness.
No being,
man or woman,
clothing, food or shelter,
alcohol or drugs,
can fill this emptiness.
For you see,
you have entered
into this universe
to connect with the Divine,
and the Divine
has no form.

Divine Love,
Truth,
Quietness,
Serenity, and Purity
are Energies
that are One
with God.

So, you can run,
you can seek
and search,
you can look,
you can battle
and manipulate,
you can control,
but you cannot win.
You can only Unite,
Join, and Be One
in The Oneness,
in the Light and Truth
of God.

You can do this if
you allow yourself
to realize your Calling.
For each and every one of you
is here
to tap into
the Love and Truth
and dwell
in the Light of God within.

God is the only Source
that promises fulfillment,
forever
and ever,
Amen.

Emptiness
Meditation

Sit and connect with the empty space within.
Do not try to fill it, control or manipulate it
to be other than what it is.
Find this empty space within.
Take three gentle breaths into this space.

At this time, let us call upon the Grace of God,
the Intelligence of the Universe,
the Absolute Perfection that exists within each and every being.

Breathe in the Light.
Breathe in Love.
Know that you are One with the Divine.
Let this empty place be nourished by the Grace of God.

War

Let there be love
in each and every soul.
May we
put down the rifles,
put down the guns.
May we open the door to Light.

As we open the door,
may we see
the sun shining
upon our fellow man,
shining upon his heart,
upon a heart
that is closed,
bitter, furious, hostile;
and worst of all
a heart that is at war.

Why war?

You, my friend,
can find the answer within.
Sit, listen to your own heart,
do your work,
let the butterfly enter to soften
and melt your heart,
to soften and dissolve

the fear, the anguish,
to soften and dissolve
all that is bitter and angry.

Where do you begin to put
an end to war?

Do you sit back and
watch the war and say
No, not me, not me,
not me.
Do you say,
No, not my son,
not my daughter.
No, not him, not her.
No, not my baby.
It can't be.
It has nothing to do with me!
Your whole life, you say no to war.
And again and again you ask, "Why war?"

My friend,
you must take the first step
to end the war,
the step toward grace.
You must take the risk
to step out of the war,
sit quietly,
go within yourself.
Then, perhaps,
you will feel the war
within you.
Then, perhaps you will

even feel the war
within
your own household.

You can only stop the war
from within.
You can stop it
from being a cancer
throughout the entire world.
All it takes
is you.

It does not take him.
It does not take her.
It does not take your leader.
It does not take your Congress.
It does not take your President
to stop war.
It takes you.
Can't you realize this?
Will you ever get the message?
Will you
ever stop the war
in your universe?

I am sorry, but out of
all the
dimensions,
you are the slowest
to learn.
You are the foggiest,
the most unclear
in your interpretation
of God and Peace.

You
lack seeing
what is present
and alive.
You
lack seeing
love and Light.

You
lack acceptance
into your own heart.
For if you
did not lack,
there would be no war.

If you fail to see,
fail to understand,
fail to comprehend,
you
will then demonstrate war
within yourself,
among your fellow man,
and in your countries.

You are like a cyclone.
You stop for a while,
get off the ride.
But then,
you ride to the top,
to the most dangerous part
of the cyclone
you possibly can.

Do I dare ask,
"Is this your lesson?"
"Is this what you must do?"
The answer is,
"No, this is not your lesson.
But, it is what you do."

Perhaps, there is another way:
If you sit quietly,
you will hear a song of grace,
and you will enter
into your heart with Love.

And as you enter, you may spiral
into a tunnel that
will take you back
to your birth,
back through that canal
you originally entered,
back to the place from which
you evolved.

If you can go back
consciously
to that place,
to that moment,
feel the energy,
then you can
renew every cell,
renew your life,
renew and embrace
every part of your being.

Then you can remember
what you need to remember.
You can remember
who you truly are.

You are not the mongrel,
you are not the destroyer,
you are not the war;
but you act as if you are.

If you put down
your weapons,
if you use
the same courage you used
to activate war,
but instead activate
your loving birth cells,
you will grow
into a more loving,
a more peaceful soul,
which will then spread love
among your fellow men and
throughout your countries,
and then you can all truly say,
"We have won."

War
Meditation

Take a deep, gentle breath.
Feel the struggle within, as you touch that place of resistance,
for distortion is in the eyes of the beholder.
Feel the war within yourself.

Take a deep, gentle breath. See yourself swimming into
the waves of peace, feel the waves of peace flowing through you.

Breathe gently and exhale. Breathe gently and exhale.
Feel the beautiful waves of peace flowing through every cell,
flowing through your mind, flowing through your whole body.
Know that you are peace. You are love. You are Divine.
Breathe gently and release. Breathe gently and release.
Keep swimming. Swim through to the other side.
Breathe gently and release.
Beneath every war, there is Peace.

The Mother

The loving mother,
the nurturing mother,
whether she is a goddess,
whether she is the mother of Mary,
whether she is your own mother,
she is the mother of peace.

In the loving mother,
you embrace the feminine,
you receive feminine energy,
as opposed to masculine energy,
and they are very different.

This is how you equalize and balance
part of your being,
by letting yourself be loved,
allowing yourself to be embraced by
the mother.
When your heart is touched
by the mother,
you will open
to a place within yourself
that you recognize
as the mother within.
Whether we are
masculine or feminine, we all
have the loving mother within.
If we do not allow ourselves

to open to the feminine grace,
we deny
an important part of ourselves.

Remember,
there is opposition in everything.
There is lightness and there is darkness,
there is good and there is bad,
there is the feminine and there is the masculine.
We carry the masculine and the feminine
in our being.
It is important to know
each and every aspect
of our entire being.
It is important
to know and embrace
the mother,
the father,
the softness,
and the strength within.

I say,
don't be afraid to feel,
don't be afraid to cry,
don't be afraid to touch,
and don't be afraid to ask.

Love.
Love.
Love.

Visualize the mother who is perfect for you,
not necessarily your birth mother,
unless you desire.

It is important
for you to feel safe in your heart.
With tender arms wrapped around you,
loving you, stay nestled
in the warmth of the feminine,
in the warmth of the mother.

The Mother
Meditation

Bring your attention to the Mother, as you embrace the child within.
Nourish that beautiful child as you visualize yourself as the Mother.

Male or female, we all have masculine and feminine energies.
If you are a female, find that nurturing place within you
and continue to embrace the child, allowing the child to feel safe.
If you are male, find the warmth within you to caress the little boy.

Breathe and exhale. Breathe and exhale,
breathing into the Mother and out through the child.
Whether the child has been hurt or damaged, scarred or loved,
love that child even more. The Mother comes in many forms.
In this meditation, you are the Mother, embracing your child.

If it is difficult for you to visualize yourself embracing your child within,
then visualize a child you know and embrace and hold
that beautiful child.

Through this meditation, you can integrate the Mother Energy with the
beautiful Divine child within.
All our lives we long for the Mother energy, for Mother love.
It is a longing that never dies.
And so, when feeling in doubt or insecure, sit in this meditation.
Let your fears melt.
Let the Mother within you, within your heart, embrace and caress
your fearful child,
for you are truly and Divinely one.

Fear

Fear causes anxiety and doubt.
Where there is fear,
there is a lack of God,
there is mistrust,
the feeling
of dropping down into a black hole.

During this moment of fear, you feel
helpless, like spinning
round and round
in a black pit.
Whatever happened to your faith,
your desire for truth, your trust?
Where did they go?

As you develop and understand
the power of the mind
and train the muscle of your mind,
you cannot fall into the pit of fear.
Fear is a lack of trust.
If you deny your fear,
try to sweep it under the rug, it will bounce back and
take on a power of its own.

But, if you wake up and face your fear,
you have a choice:

Do I choose fear
in the shadow of my doubt,
or do I choose a trusting prayer?

Dear God,
guide me, give me strength, show me the way through this day.

Fear is a choice.
Love is a choice.
So again, the work lies with you,
within you, to see, to understand and to transform.

Give the frightened child within
all the encouragement and nourishment needed,
to rebuild faith, to restore trust, to stop fear.

I do not say this is easy, but I do say it is necessary.
And so you must choose:
do you desire a life of joy, a life of richness,
or do you desire a life of fear?
You can have either one.
Which path do you choose to walk?
They are both very real.

So, embrace your life, choose life,
trust life. Do not fear to go where the fear lives.
Do not fear to face your fears.
This is the only way you can truly heal.

Blessings, Blessings,
Blessings.

Fear
Meditation

Please sit comfortably and let yourself be present
with all of your feelings, with all of your fears.

You may experience deep levels of fear.
You may not.
But, whatever you experience, know that fear is only energy,
nothing more, simply energy.

Through this meditation, your patience and willingness
will bring you through the darkness of fear and into the Light.

Now, be still and observe where the fear is located.
Be calm and sense where your fear lives;
in your mind, your heart, your body, your soul.
When you find your fear, ask,
Why fear? Why be afraid?
What is there to be afraid of?

Now, visualize a fire in front of you:
A fireplace, a fire pit, a campfire.
Watch the flames rise and dance
as you recognize your fear,
remembering that fear is only energy. It has no
power over you if you face it, see it, watch it.

Sit with your fear. Get to know it.

Now, when you have come to know your fear,
when you can name it, imagine you can
roll it into a ball and place it in both of your hands.
Then, simply throw the ball of fear into the fire.
Stay focused, follow exactly what I am saying
to you and you will have power over your fear.

Scoop up another handful of fear.
Roll it into a ball and toss it into the fire.

Scoop up another handful of fear and again,
roll it into a ball and toss it into the fire.

Do this as many times as necessary:
find your fear, name it, roll it and toss it
into the fire.
Do this until your fears are gone.

Now, breathe gently, knowing nothing can scare or rattle you.

By doing this over and over again,
you will soon come to realize, to know that
fear is just energy, powerful energy.
Your Power over fear will grow as you begin to replace your fear
with Light and Truth.

Remember, Divine Truth will move you into a more blissful,
less fearful, more loving everyday life.

Remember.

And so, I bless you for now and always.

Blessings,
blessings,
blessings and farewell.

The Miracle of the Body

We have talked about Spirit.
We have talked about Light.
We have talked about Love.

Let us now talk about the separation
of body, mind and spirit.

Your body
is a container all life flows through.
Some say the body
does not really exist.
This is true, on the spiritual level.
It is true, the body
is not Eternal or Everlasting.

But in the physical realm,
the body is very much alive
and must be nurtured,
loved and respected.

However, quite often,
when there is an illness
in the body,
you can have an attitude
that can be harmful, fearful
or destructive,
rather than having an understanding
of the body's beauty and wholeness.

This is because
you forget, lose sight
of who you really are.

Yes, there may be things you can no longer do
when you dwell in the physical body.
But you can certainly grow
and develop other aspects of Self
you never dreamed of and experience miracles.

Sometimes,
pain is the only way
one opens
to spiritual awareness.
Physical, mental and emotional pain
seem real, at the time.
But let us remember
that pain is not The Light.

However,
through the pain and fear
you may begin to desperately seek the Truth
and can then heal through The Light.

But do not think
you must be in pain
in order to see The Light.

No. No. No.

In whatever way
The Light and Truth
are shown to you,

be still and
let The Light shine
through every part of your body.
Let your body
support and serve you
in every way it can.
This is when you start to integrate body,
mind and spirit and say
Yes, to healing. Yes, to a miracle.

As you learn about pain and suffering,
you will find
there is a diamond within you
waiting to be revealed,
a diamond
reflecting The Light of Love,
The Divine Intelligence of God.

Perhaps
you will learn
from many teachers
on both the physical and spiritual plane.
And as you awaken,
you will begin to see
the distortion of your mind,
your limitations and confusions.

Then suddenly, you will find
you are
being taught
by the Greater Mind,
the Mind of God.

When you come to realize
you are
no longer a victim
of your own little mind
or thoughts,
you will be free.

So practice
seeing,
feeling
and sensing,
smelling, crying
and laughing,
and
watch yourself
flower and bloom.

All of these sensations
and emotions
are your teachers
for life.
Let them all register
as the Light
continues to shine upon you.
Look into your heart
and question,
"What is my lesson for today?"
"What do I need to know?"

Guide me,
Guide me,
Guide me.

And every day,
pray this prayer:

Prayer

Let me be
an instrument of God,
an expression of Love.
Whatever it takes
for me to awaken,
whatever it takes
for me to believe,
whatever it takes
to transform me,
show me,
teach me.

Open my heart
where it is closed,
open my mind
where there are limitations
or distortions,
free my body
so I may dance,
free the muscles in my throat
so I may sing.

Shine the Light
upon my whole being
so I may be a Light
You can see,
The Light of God
Shining Bright in me.

The Miracle of the Body
Meditation

Breathe gently and comfortably as you bring your attention to your body, checking, scanning, being very aware of your body, with each movement, in each moment.

Move your body, raise your hand, lower your hand, move your neck, circle your ankles, breathe deep, moving your stomach and chest. Stay very, very conscious of your body as your container of life, Love and The Divine Force of God. You are the container who holds the Energy. You are not the body alone.

Bring your attention to the mind.
Where is your mind?
What is your mind?
It is expansive and infinite.
Ask: "Who am I, Who am I, Who am I?"

Focus your attention on your crown chakra.
Breathe out of your crown and Beyond.
Bring Divine Information
into your body, integrating
body, mind and the Great Mind, the Great Mind of Divine Spirit.
Breathe in through your heart. Breathe out through your crown.
Where are you tight and where are you holding? Travel through your body and find the checkpoint where you can release the tightness. It is important in whatever you do, to in-
tegrate, body, mind and spirit,

for if you concentrate only on your physical body, with all its constraints and complex energies, dark energies, tight energies, negative energies, you will then create
dis-ease.

Understand, the Greater Mind, the Divine Mind, can free and heal your body. If you learn to swim in your energy, fly, soar in your energy, you will be a shining star.
You will be a free floating star.

Once again, focus attention on your body, breathing in and breathing out. Breathing in and breathing out.

Bring the attention to your Third Eye, which allows you to expand into greater ways of thinking, as you exercise the Third Eye and open the pineal gland.

Breathing in and breathing out. Breathing in and breathing out.

Once again, bring your attention to your crown chakra, which is your path to heaven. Breathing in through your Third Eye and breathing out through your crown chakra,
releasing everything, all the way.

Spiraling back into your body, take a deep and gentle breath into your heart chakra, breathe into your Third Eye, and breathe out through your crown. Breathing out through your crown, into the Ether, circling and spiraling back into the body, as you integrate
body, mind and spirit.

As you come to practice this more and more, as you learn to sing, dance and fly, you are integrating. You are integrating all of you. You are inte-grating and becoming greater than you can ever imagine. Through this practice, I promise you, you will soar in time. You will come to intuitively know and understand more, be more in touch so a Divine healing can take place in your body and your mind as you let Spirit heal you.

Come back into the body.
See where you are in pain. It is not to be ignored. It is not to be denied.
It is to be recognized. It is to be loved. So, take the pain and the fear, anxiety and tension and embrace it all.
Embrace and transform it, transform it with Pure Loving Energy
and Acceptance.
Through acceptance, miracles happen, healing happens,
in a split second.

So, I ask you, through your heart, through your anxiety, through your illness, through your discomfort, to practice, practice, practice.
Become the best you can be on all levels of
body, mind and spirit.

Blessings and farewell, as you fly high.

A Thank You from Isram

I want to thank all of you for allowing yourselves to open,
for just a moment, for just a second, for just a breath.
If there was just one lesson, one meditation, one word
that touched or moved you,
know you have opened to your own reflection of Love,
you have seen the Essence
of your Genuine Divine Being,
and I thank you for this opening.

And so, as you continue to grow, as you continue to flower,
as you continue to move on in life
and expand your Being,
your work, your prosperity, remember,
there are no limitations.
There is only great abundance in everything.
All is possible.
Every dream, every thought, every idea, every possibility
is available to you.

As you flourish and move on through your life,
as you radiate and glow, manifest and expand,
I ask you to accept the deepest parts of your Divine Essence.

I leave you with this one last meditation.
As you flower and blossom into
the greatest human being you can be,
as you recognize the Great Spirit that exists within and Beyond
I bless you for
now and always.

In love,
Isram

The Yellow Rose
Meditation

As you come to your Meditation,
sit comfortably rather than lying down. In this way Energy
will flow strong within and your attention will be sharp.

Take deep, gentle breaths into your heart chakra,
not into your physical heart, but into the heart center,
the center of your compassion and love.
Keep your focus on your heart chakra as you gently inhale and exhale.
Concentrate. Focus on this place within.

As you sit in stillness, envision yourself in a beautiful
rose garden. See a tiny yellow rosebud
being placed in the center of your heart.
See this rosebud blooming and blossoming in the quiet center
of your being.

With each inhalation and exhalation, see this rose slowly opening.
Do not force the rose to open.
Do not push, or force or try.
Just watch this rose.

Stay with the rose until you see it open into full bloom.
Smell the fragrance of the rose as you sit with this rose
in your open heart.

Now bring your attention to the roots. Sense the roots of the rose growing down into the rich soil, then move gently up the stem and once again, see the fullness and beauty of the rose in full bloom.

You are now one with the essence of the beauty of the yellow rose blooming forever in your body, mind, spirit, and beyond.

May you be blessed in the Garden of Peace forever and ever.

About Mara Joyce Chapel

Mara Joyce Chapel is a gifted channel for the loving spirit, "Isram," who defines himself as a "master teacher of light."

Through Mara, Isram's love, wisdom, and strength have become a source of spiritual growth for countless people. For over thirty years, Isram has guided seekers to reflect on their innate gifts, untapped potential, and their Higher Selves, enabling them to manifest their dreams from a place of truth and compassion.

Isram's wisdom goes deep into our spirits and psyches and connects to our "Memory Cells," which are responsible for our thought patterns and belief systems. As Isram gently penetrates these cells, they become more receptive, and like a sponge, we absorb new ideas and vibrations. As this new life force integrates into our daily lives, we are better able to manifest our innate spiritual gifts and talents.

Mara has been privileged to offer the teachings and gifts of Isram to people of all walks of life, including doctors, teachers, therapists and healers. Some of Mara's clients include Pat Rodegast, Emmanuel's Book; Kenneth R. Kafka, M.D., "Integrative Medicine", Beverly Hills, CA; Mitchell L. Gaynor, M.D., "Integrative Oncologist", Presbyterian Hospital, NY and author of Gene Therapy; Barry Manilow, singer-songwriter and producer, and actress Renee Taylor.

Mara's teachers include Ram Dass, Steven Levine, Rosalyn Bruyere, Emile Conrad Da'oud, Judith Schmidt, Ph.D., Jack Kornfield, Joseph Goldstein, Kyabje Kalu Rinpoche, Barbara Brennan, Marianne Williamson, Shakti Gawain, and her master teacher, Isram.

For further information, contact Mara Joyce Chapel at mjchapel@aol.com

Made in the USA
Columbia, SC
03 June 2018